AS NIGHT FADES INTO LIGHT

AS NIGHT
FADES
INTO LIGHT

Poetic Ponderings

MONA KRISTENSEN

Pot of Gold Publications

Copyright

Contents

DEAD OF NIGHT

DAWN

DUSK

I

Good Owl Wisdom

When lost in a dark wilderness:
Turn on your sharp night vision

Steer clear of dangerous predators
or creatures with wounded instincts

Brush ticks off fast before nasty
diseases have a chance to infect you

Soar high above the scene to get
the Bird's Eye perspective

Good Owl Wisdom

When lost in a dark Wilderness:

-Turn on your sharp Night Vision

*-Steer clear of dangerous Predators
or Creatures with wounded instincts*

*-Brush Ticks off fast before nasty
diseases have a chance to infect you*

*-Soar high above the scene to have
the Bird's Eye perspective*

Battlefields

I just want to be free, I said,
free to do what I want
Child, the struggle's made by your mind,
that's what makes it so crafty and unkind

I just want to feel free, I sighed,
free to live how I need
Child, uncover what freedom means to you:
disoriented and drained by years of inner war

I just want to be free, I sobbed;
free to be who I am

Child, let go of the unfruitful fight:
freedom's waiting within, go reclaim your right

When this is over: this war with roots in the past
My life will surely fit me; truly fit me at last

I just want to be free

3

Beautiful Deception

Love, seeing with your eyes I surrendered,
only to find myself smaller than before
My secret curse found me once more

Thought I'd fled but got caught again,
there's no escaping a spell from within
A slumbering bomb waiting to go off
Silenced, but still not disarmed
It awaits my slow recovery
to do its terminal harm

Oh, what a beautiful deception

4

Just Breathe

Sun rises but I can't see,
is it dawning in front of me?
Just breathe - keep breathing

Sunshine or blinding snow;
frozen silence has nothing to show
Just breathe – keep breathing

Nothing to do, no one to be
Simple as a withering tree
Just breathe – keep breathing

Leave every illusion behind
It was all but a trick of the mind
Just breathe – keep breathing

Anytime now, the missing piece
will return back home to me
Probably.... probably

Just breathe

5

A Stranger

A stranger, after the fall
No me means no problems
Yet someone is troubled
in these haunted halls
Nothingness is holy,
is what I was told,
while the absence echoes
through a dreamer cold
I yearn to be real
but somehow I'm not
Ghostly, still and frozen
The blinds remain shut

6

Griefances

Love leaves me smaller
That's not what I was told,
that's not what I was sold

I want my money back

Love leaves me weaker
It's not what they promised
Love's mark always missed

I want my money back

Love is safest on the inside
As soon as it touches the world
it's corrupted, co-opted, a gnarl

I want my money back

My love is safe with me!

Is love safe with me?

7

A Pattern of Leaves

Last week I had a dream

You were directing a music video
in royal but old-fashioned theater
I was merely one of the extras
following angry instructions

You told us in moody manners
how to arrange leaves on the floor
Even long after the awakening,
it somehow stayed with me

8

Petrified Tree

Past voices come and go,
they amplify and then recede
in an everchanging ebb and flow
beyond any human control

A cacophony of familiar phrases
take root in mind and senses can,
and weigh down a weakened will:
words are seeds, I understand

Cherishing old ancestral tools,
or worshipping drops of the sea,
clinging to petrified trees' remedy
will only ever make us fools

Stuck in a morass of messages
Overtaken by paralyzing fright
Until a whispered life-affirming Yes,
has a force, a holy fire, ignite

Personal Notes

Personal Notes

Personal Notes

DEAD OF NIGHT

9

A Wordless Weight

Once, a long time ago,
the girl pulled at his sleeve

He looked down and
told her in unspoken words:

You've got to get up yourself
Your neediness makes me sick
Your show of affection is undignified
You've got to learn to help yourself
To follow your bliss or desire is bad
Love is a burden, unsellable waste

Loyalty and money matter most

I'll make time to be there for you
when there is nowhere left to run

Cozy Cage

Life in a bright and cozy cage
is pretty and peaceful yet cold
Outside disturbances don't interfere
when pleasantly left all alone

No locked or bolted doors,
no spiked windows, iron bars
A sunray through blinds reveals
habitual ghosts kept on guard

Tired songbird's about to retire,
by now has perfected her scheme
No fence or alarm is required
for treasures remaining unseen

Hibernating Heart

My heart is hiding in secret places,
trembling and scarred from old lost cases

I try to restore it by long-distance means,
hoping miracles spring from silver screens

A thousand ties keep holding it back;
innocent victim of a choir of cruel attacks

Tell me how to silence them and finally be free
though please not all: the tenderest one is holy

12

Mother Mirage

In a morphed mirror you'll see:
familiar figures dancing around
to past tunes and rhymes

In a morphed mirror you'll see:
An old scene with no movement,
frozen in place and time

In a morphed mirror, you'll see:
dear old friends pulling back
as you cry out or call

In a morphed mirror, you'll see:
no recognition, lack of reflection,
slices of self, a soul's fall

Misconceived
Misgivings.
Misread,
Missing
Amiss

13

Days of Darkness

In days of darkness
and hours of despair
I rest each night time
with your voice in ear
Powerlessly patient
I witness the drama
unraveling before me:
the remnants of karma
One day, I envision,
when all this is through,
my heart's true desire:
I'm resting with you

Sisterhood of Little

On Sundays,
My sisters and I
frequently pay visits
to a nearby supermarket;
driven to a home-like locus
with lots of parking

In the church of
an incredible Big Deal
we worship the God in power;
led to market and taught
as our sisters before us,

how to measure up
and be littled

We trade precious
time, energy and love
for plotted plants of plastic
to decorate our cozy cages
with artificial artifacts
and gratefully
call it home

At the cash counter
We receive a small change
and celebrate our trade-offs
with outstanding hopeful hearts,
carrying bags of tidbits
out sliding doors

Back in the kitchen
we compare expendables
and prepare a festive meal:
pink shrimps and toast
one another for this
familiar fortune

Almighty provider
enable your deprived daughters
to break a spell caused by
being on the breadline,
or way below another,
for far too long

Rewild our essence
of tender, fierce, and free
trade cups of worth, of being well
for each fool's gold plated,
man-made trophy
we were ever sold

15

Chronic Fatigue

My purse is full of lack
in absence of You

My limbs are log-like
in absence of You

My muscles are aching
in absence of You

My body is weaker
in absence of You

My skin turns to rash
in absence of You

My mind gets a mist
in absence of You

My vision impaired
in absence of You

My heart's trembling
in absence of You

My soul falls apart
in absence of You

16

Blue Butterfly

My heart feverishly flutters
like wings on a little blue butterfly
caught in an ever-so-tiny construct
modeled out of scraps and ruins

17

Fallow Fruit

From a certain distance
my garden looks minute
Shallow eyes miss out on
riches of ripened fruit

A closer gaze reveals
organic crop in bounties
Sweet and juicy goodies
drop from crooked trees

Heavy branches bend,
pointing toward roots
while fallen fruit decay;
recycling back in loops

Your intended dwells
within an apple core
for final harvest home:
a lost girl, never more

Personal Notes

Personal Notes

Personal Notes

DAWN

18

Shielded

When you fear you have lost everything;
inner peace, joy and love: your true self
Then it dwells, safe within you, still
where once hidden away in a shell*

*Epilogue from "What's the Matter with Maria?"

19

Autonomous Heart

What others applaud
the heart may ignore,
and movements of many
create but a pause

Obey but a true call,
even delayed on repeat
by the blood that leaves it
through circuits obsolete

Follow your own beat,
or foreign friendly faces
Silent, slow, yet steady
to secret, sacred places

20

Higer Love

My love keeps growing tall,
hands may never reach him
He suddenly took off while
I stayed good and small

I watch each twist and turn
with genuine excitement
Proud to see his wingspan
and just the slightest yearn

Half-starved, I listen closely
to nourishing notes he sings
Still longing for reunion
in spite of broken wings

If ever he should ponder
the origin of these sparks
I whisper to stay present
at dawning after dark

Ladder of Thorns

I slept in the dark
in an invisible thorn bush
engaged in most trivial things

No real movements,
keeping almost still there
to avoid any stings on my skin

The sun, ever insistent
awoke downhearted dreamer,
wiping the sleep from her eye

Sharp rays revealed
thorny triggers everywhere
Oh, look at the beautiful bright sky!

Climbing on thorns
is an ascent full of ache
- those pains lessen with time

At the end of it,
your whole world awaits,
fragrant, vibrant, affecting - alive!

22

Taste for Sweetness

I've got a taste for sweetness
It gets me every day
This craving for a substance
to pull me out of bed

My sweet tooth is relentless:
wants more and more and more
Won't settle for dilutions,
just honey nectar pure

I clamber high and low,
chasing an ever-flowing well
of liquid golden goodness
to fill my thirsty cells

One day I will unearth it
No stone is left unturned
And when it's so - my promise:
present it to the world

23

Body Buddha

In an ideal, unspoiled world,
we would know to only say yes
when wholeheartedly feeling it
and no when really meaning no
However, simply sensing what is true
and to somehow express it, is good for us,
signaling to our sensitive sensory system,
that we hear and acknowledge its truth
and will stand up for ourselves, our safety

Trust the wisdom of your whole, sentient being:
it loves you and wishes you nothing but the best

24

Powers to be

For ages, I used my power
to give it away

Not losing belonging
but losing my bearings,
I traded empowered
for impoverished

Identification passed down
for safety and security
as a rule of thumb for
countless reasons

Frequently, powerless
is our first given name
Though keeping it so
is dangerous

Designated to disown powers
sacrificed in the name of love,
or in the name of fear

By and by
By bloodline
By gender
By trauma
By tears

Oceans of tears

Today,
I gently wipe my eyes,
stand on my own two feet,
calmly reclaiming
my true name

25

Riches, underlying

On my humble plot,
in my tiny little garden,
half of the premise is pebbled
Stones, for a century cemented by
many stoic, hardworking men

A good gardener prevents
wild seeds from taking root,
meticulously micromanaging
signs of unreasonable unruliness,
heavy-handedly removing shoots

For the longest time
I forcefully fought away
wild-growing, shameless seeds
from entering my bare and barren,
coarse-grained courtyard

Oh, heart's a flower child
envisioning enchanted meadows,
buying bouquets from early in May
At the last call, I saw the dawning light
and simply let Nature have her way

26

Clowns or Gardeners?

You tend to equate me:
frozen still helplessness,
enraged burning skulls
or showers of water from
a despairing girl's eyes

I tend to equate you
to chilling echoes of
loving words unspoken,
arms never embracing,
eyes not truly seeing

Let us re-learn to be,
before fathers' control or neglect,
before any smothering hands
Be who we are beyond
old abuse or rejection

Let us tend to be Love
in our most fertile garden,
running nowhere as the sun
slowly illuminates every
clouded, quivering bud

27

Dear Animus

You keep telling me
I have work to do,
mountains to climb

I answer that
as inner mountaineers,
loving one another right
seems the paramount part of
our job description

28

Vision at Daybreak

An endless winter left my fields barren
but for frost-flowers waiting for thaw
when, at last, timing is right

The era that welcomes all beings of life
without archaic distinctions,
untangled from fright

A garden in bloom, arched by a rainbow,
wonderfully weird hearts rapture
in warmth of the sun

Loving presence pours into our souls,
transforming old divisions:
we're finally whole

29

Reversed Requirements

Truths I was never told

I have to follow my heart
I have to be my real, true, full self
I have to feel free to express myself
I have to be appreciated for being here
I have to have my needs acknowledged and met
I have to thrive to consistently give of myself
I have to listen to and take good care of my body
I have to tune into, honor & obey my Soul's call

Personal Notes

Personal Notes

Personal Notes

DAYLIGHT

30

Evidence

False evidence appears to bury
eternal love in hopeless ground
While howling apparitions circle
blazing flames of life around

I call on heaven, oh why
ignite a sleeping heart's desire
if but to quench and diminish
its gentle, nourishing fire?

My skin forever burns in battle
to decide on a sacred cause at last
Inside a soft and silent whisper:
knowing Truth is not of past

Am I muse, spiritual mistress,
co-creator or God's work of art
Muddled mind and hungry body
steady, ever humbler heart

31

Love Lessons

In summertimes, it happens,
grasping fruit of unripe essence
to linger in tender young love
and sweet, reclining presence

A tree got marked, disfigured
by immature, opposing forces
Tiny, fragile sprouts crushed
under hoofs of blinkered horses

Some declare: follow your bliss,
but remember in future be wise
Is before you the love you lost
or a familiar mirror, disguised?

This time no rifts or regrets
Our love is sound and secure
Learn your lessons by heart
Soul recognizes its own core

True beloved is finally home,
for years his lady has longed
Springtime's about to arrive
in singing our jubilant song

32

A knowing

Soft tones behind the veil
Music from another plane
calling, calling out my name,
yet fading into doubt again

Please stay a little longer,
just a little longer,
this time around

Like a million diamonds
washing upon inner shores,
illuminating remains of night,

merging us to the One before

Please stay a little longer,
just a little longer,
this time

Because I know now;
know your real name

Because I know now;
know my real name

I know

33

Reunion

Distant calls and silent howl
Strikes a chord in parted soul

Love seems safest from afar
Out of reach, but somehow near

Close enough to warm a heart
Precious as the finest art

Truthful words and tender stare
Heal this split and love is here!

34

Eternal Eden

Waves upon waves of showers
sweep through ancient garden
Forces beyond any human will
cause rapid shifts in weather
Light and later, heavy, rain
Stormy to windy; then still
See the seasons come and go,
temperature rises and falls as
sun burns off dead and diseased
One singular seedling prevails
in our Eternal Eden where
frost no longer means freeze

35

Anchoring

At night, there's a mean old monkey
between us in bed, playing games

Today, let's rub the sleep off our eyes,
and start fanning this sacred flame

I am not ashamed of obeying it at all,
forever found love the highest of calls

We don't have to leave anyone in remorse,
as steadily anchoring this heaven of ours

But do take time to heal and fully recover
Standing by in faith, I know your power

Losing you once more, I could not bear
Beloved: you are more than welcome here

36

Healing a Child

What does it take
to heal the child within?
To mend her sorrows,
to raise his chin?

We chase the same
through different means:
belonging, be valued,
feel heard and seen

We cleanse our Soul,
to absolve former fail,

reluctantly trusting
that love will prevail

We need the same,
no bad can befall,
if seeing each other
as not other at all

We are the same,
our healing is done
A miracle happens
when two see as one

37

All I ever Wanted

All I ever wanted was to carry you
like a badge of honor on my chest
wherever I went, to proudly display
your countless virtues and gifts

All I ever wanted was to dress myself
in nothing but united fabrics of love,
baring a soul while completely at ease
Certain about our rightful place in it all

All I ever wanted was to create in peace
No secrets to keep: true - openhearted
Such simplicity, such pure expressions
At last and forever living unguarded

38

Ode to My Beloved

Whenever you join me
my empty pen runnet over,
and words flow unbounded
in an upward rising surge

Terrain left untended:
arid fields during a dry spell,
awakens to live and luster
by our sweet water well

I figure without you
these half-hearted toils
would likely go back to
yield nothing at all

Now, a steadied arrow
hits bulls eyes with ease
The Archer smiles softly,
lets out a sigh of relief

39

Oil of Life

I was starving for so long,
circling on familiar ground,
eating crumbs coming my way
- lead astray or to be found?

Adrift toward surrogate honey,
a clouded eye often goes blind
Until the sweetest, truest tones
summon lost ones home again

You are my Oil of Life
Soul thirsts for steady flows
A wasteland without the nectar
that re-ignites immortal glow

40

Worldwide Witchcraft

What if our worst sins
are in truth our sicknesses?
Our wounds and contortions:
the injuries least aligned
with everything Divine

What if we are all witches?
Forever, for better or worse
Willfully or unwillingly
but mainly unwittingly

Stirring an old soup of
unconscious ingredients
Casting out our shadows,
conjuring up nightmares

Repeating patterns
Rehashing dogmas
Recreating dramas,
traumas - karma

Let's be brave - begin inside
Heal all of our hurting children
Turn a contaminated minefield
to a lush, flowering meadow

Re-generate and create anew:
One whole world of wonder

Micro Macro Mirror

Does the world serve as a mirror,
reflecting our shadow and light?
So, we are able to see the whole:
delight in the blessed, the beauty
or find a way to mend our souls

Past hurt and harmful voices
show up in different disguises
until we're no longer triggered

As old wounds are healed,
these pain points dissolve,
troubled situations resolve

Be open and ready to learn
but let go of crippling self-doubt:
always second-guessing yourself

No, have faith in the spark of life
and honor what's true in your heart

Your maker then bows before you:
a divine creation can finally start

42

Divine Validation

Dearest Child

You are loved and respected without having to do anything to deserve it.

We understand everything that goes on inside you: intense emotions, every twinge of a feeling.

Your thriving heart and health, your happiness and full freedom are our no. 1 priority.

We demand nothing from you and delight in all of your authentic expressions.

What you give freely from your true self is deeply appreciated.

We celebrate, cherish and honor your innocent soul.

43

Illuminated Heart's Creed

I AM the love I long for

There's nothing I have to do
to deserve this: my Birthright
All I need is to remember Truth

True love is the foundation of:
Joy, Peace, Creativity & Freedom

Wholeness is Holiness
As I embrace all aspects of self
the Sacred Heart illuminates

44

Heartlights

As dated defenses defrost,
melting set snowflakes of past
Mirasols miraculously birth:
Heartlights shining on Earth*

*Epilogue from "Who's Maria again?"

Personal Notes

Personal Notes

Author Bio

Mona Kristensen is a Danish author: an intuitive writer passionate about raising awareness. She has a keen eye for the subtle ways in which Life speaks to us and a big heart for healing our inner child: the most sensitive, expressive and imaginative part of us; a part which sadly often ends up wounded or repressed.

Through her writing, she hopes to mend a bit of this unfortunate damage.

Website: www.monakristensen.com